Eugene Vesey was born and brought
was educated at a Roman Catholic grammar school in
Manchester, a Roman Catholic seminary in the English Lake
District, at the University of Manchester, where he read
English Language and Literature, and then at the University of
Liverpool, where he did his teacher training. He lives and
works in London, where he is a lecturer in English as a
Foreign Language at a College of Further Education. He has
also written two novels, **Ghosters**, published by Spire,
available from amazon.co.uk, and **Opposite Worlds**,
available from amazon.com. This is his first book of poetry.

VENICE

AND

OTHER POEMS

Eugene Vesey

for

John Barber

thanks

a stone in the water

creeping morning-soft into the chamber of my mind
visions distant intolerant of trespass
bestowing their brief benedictions and retiring
intangible as incense fumes to the crypts
the secret vaults where i can never follow
nocturnal

winding wreaths around the grey and crumbled pillars
of my soul which waits solitary on
these empty hills spurning burial straining for
the bugle of some saviour the echo promised
with the birth of time that time would pass away
vespertine

that then light would be the light blooming at the centre
truth to gather and fremescent sweep and swoop
submerging all the vain extensions washing the world
of her iniquities her crooked harvest raze
and sow her purged fields with dreams to dawn
matutinal

a walk in the rain

the rain falls
and compelled by some inner compulsion
i walk the grey suburban streets
tracts of grey shining concrete
wind folding its wet mantle
around the tame suburban trees
an uncouth stranger
assailing their virgin charm
and I am reminded of the lion
stalking the fleet beauty of
piteous gazelles on some green parkland
in deepest nearest Africa
my heart goes out to those sad creatures
(i know they will never make their claim
on my distant pity
and that perhaps this journey will be
the last crowded lonely journey
of their lives …)

to where I ask quite simply
are *we* running
and i pray that we are not
as i suspect
running from darkness to darkness
from dust to dust
from ash to ash
i pray to the darkness and to the dust
that this be not so
lux aeternum approach and fire
the cold cloisters of my soul –
for who will hear the candle else
where the night of truth has dawned
(do i hear tenebral chanting
from her dim tabernacle?)

in remote fear i turn the neatly-pointed
suburban corners and eat the rain
for does not the devil like a roaring lion
go about seeking whom he may devour
and is he not united hypostatically
with the zebra crossing?
and may he not be staring stealthily
from among the trim topiary?
yes there is no cause to dispense
oneself from the fear of forces unknown
but whose stories have been told –
i genuflect to the mystery
i absolve myself of bravery

and take to premeditated flight
for thus will i cover most ground
salvation is an immunizing drug
security uncomfortably close
to the borders of self-satisfaction
i plumb for the open plain
am exhilarated to be one
of the hunted ones
though there be no sight of the hunter
and after all the earth and grass
must remain my god my beginning my end
my final resting place

the brash advertisements are whipped
by the wind sharply from their resting places
pabulum for oppressed minds other than mine
one or two leaves revel in the wind
i bow my head
for I am touching the spirit of Christ
my finger-tips moistened
in the current of his truth
my unfathomable privilege

the smart new pinewood-faced church
i pass quickly chasing arrogance
from my disillusion
for i have found that the church is
the shroud of Christ
that he lives in flesh and blood
that dirt and poverty and disease
hunger and blindness are
his sanctuary lamps

over the big sweep of bridge I pass
reflecting wryly on these thoughts
and forge on resisting the lure
of the heaving river below
fearing I might hear there if I dwell
the lion's forest roar

Alley Cat

The city is like a corpse full of microbes
On this foggy, damp evening;
The pavements are cold to touch and clammy,
The great empty warehouses
Stare out eyelessly into the sky;
The streets are clogged with neon-drowned people
Crawling back into the night-time,
The time of remembrance and forgetting;
In the dim alleyway
The jade eyes of the cat confront you
And tell you to go away –
This is no place for the dead;
The sickly lamplight floods you and says
This is no place for darkness;
And so the city streets re-swallow you
As you swim back to your harbour,
But a policeman stands by the door,
Like a death-watch beetle.

An Old Irish Peasant Woman

She is old, huddled in black,
Wrinkly-faced and silver-haired;
Her hands, as rough as peat,
Have sown a hundred harvests,
And opened a thousand gates;
Her feet, as fragile as twigs,
Have tripped a hundred miles or more
Along the looping, lazy country lanes;
Her eyes rested on these fields when
They knew only the horse's solemn plod,
Not the lumbering assault of tractors,
Beetling bronchial and garrulous;
Outside her wooden cottage door,
The abandoned plough lies,
A rusted relic condemned to death,
Waiting grass-graved for resurrection,
Silent, usurped, sullen iron skeleton,
Rejected, ignored, symbol of decay.

She has been touched by a hundred summers,
When summers were slow and lingering,
Watched the flowers come and go,
The falling of a hundred snows
And the revival of a hundred springs;
Spent long, lonely hours bending on the bog,
Among the heather that blooms out there still;
But now inside the whitewashed cottage,
With its flag-stoned floor and dusty windows,
As dark and dim as a mausoleum,
She rocks to and fro on her creaky rocking-chair,
Her eyes romancing in the spluttering flames,
Leafing through her pressed and precious memories.

Anhaga

Along the shadow edge of the old story,
Where strange lights prod my mind,
Strange familiar winds creep across my back,
There I feel the taut heartstretch,
The baffle and bend of being's weight;
I have been compacted to irrelevancy
Between the mills of science and history,
I have been weaned, my brain filleted –
The moon so suddenly turned to rock
And my heart driven back to earth!

In the mine of me I crawl, timorous mole,
Surfacing always to the blasted vista
Where are buried so many faiths and friends,
While the dead stars shine on.

I will not rise again –
The foot of the tree is no haven,
It rains blood there
And the white dove stares down with glassy eye;
The great finger swings through space,
My world dangles in my cranium
And will be buried with me,
An everlasting funeral knell,
Toll of toy hope, now it dangles …

And knowing me,
I will wind through the galaxies
And parachute onto a heaven
Crowded with crosses!

Annihilation

Through smog-smitten city they scuttle,
   Scores of roads and rattle of railway train,
   Through brick-block and brawl of belling traffic,
Faces engraved with alarm of time and
Swirl about their fast feet, while with white hands
   They pluck fate and forward flee, flicker and fail
   Into the swoop of night.

Ride the roll of racing time, run the marathon
   And the reel of ragged reef unravelling them,
   Ride the rodeo and buck of hurricane hearts;
And when the tide looms, clipping sunlight,
Shoots up their shivered backs, shoals them,
   Further and further they fall and flail
   Into the nought of night.

Apex

Light glows fluorescent
From her skull
In the ultraviolet moon;
She is dissolved within,
Her particles collide
Behind curtains of blood;
Bliss deflects from
Her lightning-fused nerves,
A billion nights break
On the strand of her heart,
Strewn with starshells:
The universe shrinks to
A pearly grain within her brain
Herself within.

But she craves the freedom of death!
A tempest of tears
Drives her to her shelter;
Her tears turn to hail,
Her blood to sleet
In the grinding wind,
And she is subsumed,
Magnet of clay reclaims;
While the leaves pile around,
She is hammered, heartbeat, home to earth.

Autumn

To you and all those fallen angels
Whose spirits invest the woodlands
In most golden autumn when
The trees and leaves and coy streamlets
Are varnished with a falling sun
Its parting benediction gently lain
With technicolour fingers.

Your night has come your season
Of discontent hustling you away
Adamant and cold as death
With ice in its veins hands of drear cold
Marshy breath and
No music in its heart.

And I who have tended your rites
Abided with you and at your darkest hours
Infused the homage of my kindred soul
I am left now to mourn in sorrow
The ashes of your mystery
And wonder –

Where have you gone
What resting place could take
The burden of bones so venerable
What sanctuary enchamber the passing
Of a beauty such as yours?
And I am moved to hope that you were indeed
The harbinger of paradise.

birdy

the sun weeps on the windows
and the rain shines
over the flatlands
orchids hustle in the wind
and distance is quashed
with puff of sweaty cloud

estuaries of dead wet trees
with damp fingers scratch
the greenhouse roof
and cobs of sodden bark stray the lawn
an unstrung wren is pounded
by the swaying storm

typhoons of years moments ripped cell by cell
blanketing the flatlands
combs of spawn spawn of lifelessness
settle in the marrows of my limbs
creep into the bays of my arms

carry away the trophies of my memory
strip me and take me back to wild seas
through ragged sheets and moon-filled sails
the bullion of my brains the hoops that bind me
to myself in the lightless hour of being

chirrup and hop chirrup and spring
brown pestered thing
alight upon your raft of destiny
it will take you there
back where you belong
with the rest of us

so gulp the storm while you may
bang your beak on the stone wall
throw up your wings in dismay
and await no other day

Blades

The past breathes like fire
On my shivering neck
Chilling my spine
Battening on the blood
Of inescapable memories
Vampire dreams
At my birth I crawled forth
From the rock of war
Life exploded within me
And I was shocked to despair
I lay upon the forest floor
And through the grid of hell I gaped
From light to light I stumbled
Until darkness overtook me
The poison bloomed within my heart
But I race on with fearful heart
Life's escalator back to the future
The blades whirring
About my frightened heels

blind man's bluff

i put the photos back in the book
square films of life gone by
in those shiny skins those dead faces
sound a thousand notes of joy and loss
victims even then of time the spade
time the demon artist
black hand that works by night and day
in the factory of our fates
time the ripper

but a smile cannot die
a child's joy or birth of good love
such perhaps are the angels
and heaven is a moment snatched
from time's ogrish grasp
oh the stars in our dark souls!

do stars escape the executioner?
and if i don't make heaven after all
perhaps i won't be sore
that it was once so far away inside
so near away outside
through mountains of worms and flames
always in hell's fist

and all i know is that love and sorrow
must have collected somewhere

Blue Sky Pie

Blue sky
In my eye,
Why, oh why,
Must we die?
But I'd die
Without a sigh,
If to die
Meant that I
Could simply fly
Up to that sky,
This earth defy,
Dissolve on high ...

burning an old photo

the tree on the hill burns
as the photo curls and browns
the house is burning down
where we spent such happy days
now she writhes and squirms
and disappears before my eyes
our love lies in ashes
i feel as if i've killed her
but she was already dead

Christ

The blackberry is crushed between my fingers
The juices of a bitter June run through them;
The holy waters of life have turned to grit
In my memory, there's nothing pure any more
And my soul is stained with the blood of Christ.

Oh Christ, you have died not for me but on me,
Died twice and deserted me;
You were ten-thousand years to me
And now you are ten-thousandth of a second, gone.

Collapse

My dreams are cobwebs now,
Among the blackened rafters
Of my haunted mind.
There dwells spectral silence
And I stare in silence across
The graveyard of my memory
Where so many souls lie dead.
Now I have the mantle of solitude,
The dignity of dereliction in which
To ponder my destination,
Perhaps to reach for new happiness.
But no more will I turn
To the architect of my sadness,
Or look to the skies for angels' voices:
Now my only joy is a vision
Through a mirror – wild wind on deep water –
Of what might have been.

coming back from the bog

steel-rimmed wheels grinding
over the stones in the lane
tumbril of turf bouncing
above the hedge

over on the lime-crops
white cabin bonneted with straw
snoozing in the sun
piping turf smoke

beneath the crumbling bridge
river dawdling
hammered with sunlight tree-tressed
gin-bright over the stones

fish slapping the water
lifting a shower of jewellery
ripple of silence
curtains the world

dawn

the weevil burrows has dribbled to
   the very flower of this thor's day
perambulatory centipede trailing
   his mean and ugly tinsel
across the stoop oogh pidder wiley
   westward wiz and my fingers spider
chilly the glass milk
   which unlike me knoweth the night's
encephalograms if the night has cells

time for matins chaunt the nidiferous
   chancelmongers abicker in the gutter
draping delicate invisibles between
   walls and telegraphs
and sky is fresh as milk frothed and clean
   pin-bright intangible as a fairy
clouds mushing doglike nose to nose
   yap yap
slough of blue beautiful
   and gently fall away
      faintly gale away

somewhere up there life cool morning
   breezes winnowing my hair and
drawing silk seas of cool over
   the reefs of my body morning moving
inspectorial around me sniffing
   the wide morning unchorded
great lazybones as sure of resurrection
   as i of somewhere up there life

where i raise my hands to touch
   stretch unpeel sleep and unbury
to a new day savouring wisps of woodsmoke
   acrackle aday cockadoodle day

dead of morning

in march i heard the hard wind
stammering its manic message
upon the shore sound in sound
with the hoarse-throated sea
the groaning waters engraving
an everlasting song of sorrow
on the shingle

and somewhere in the morning vault
i glimpsed the sailing silver-winged gulls
white ghosts wailing in the dawn-harsh sky
voices that said that i would die
i felt the sea lick coldly at my face
the wind's wintry fingers
searching for my soul

death

to be born for ever in this instant
transcendent essence of all dreams
sublime being where no oceans thrash
no stars peek or winds rasp
and all voices are blent with the seas'
faraway lullaby –
you are all glitter
fluorescent ecstasy of otherness
untimed, unfleshed, dissolved
into nothingness

now all books are pulp
oceans furl back
the earth a marble
lost in space
as you fly away

you are darkness burning bright
all heart and hands and liquid
bliss of mind, thousand shimmering
shocks, electric heaven, black bliss

all prayers are redundant now
comic echoes, God a mask
in the rubble of my dreams

death creeps up like a wolf
and dismantles all of us
while the buzzard wheels above
waiting for the crumbs

defeat

the cortege in white
moves slowly through
the congealed blackness
carrying the shroud
wherein lies the unnailed body
of their dead friend

this funeral has lasted
two thousand years
though many of the mourners
went away despondently
long long ago
gentle ghosts who lost their way

i lifted back the shroud with love
to touch his cold sad face
but there was nothing there
they told me he had gone
back to Gethsemani
to start again

and never came back

Despair

The children dance upon the shore,
Before the sea's silent voltage;
The sand is dim, waves are silver shadows,
The children's moonstruck figures
Dance softly slowly miming
The sad mystery of
Their unchosen fate.

Their eyes are unseeing, reflecting
A million stars above,
Dream galaxy beyond their reach;
There are candles in their hands,
They want to walk on water
To another land, some star to shine
Upon their lonely night;
They cannot speak, their mouths gape,
Echo the silence in their souls.

The night is still, the sea is calm,
As the spectral shadows dumbly dance;
Their palms try to push the darkness back
As they tread the sand in circles
And mutely pray in deep despair
For dawn, for light of day.

Suddenly they stop their garish dance
And pause – a pale light is glowing in the sky,
The waves are whispering music in their ears,
Sun is rising before their blinking eyes!
They throw their candles into the sea,
They cheer, they laugh, at last they're free.

But suddenly comes a crack of thunder,
Like the booming of a giant gun;
It's the voice of God, guffawing as
He switches off the light again.

diminuendo

where the hewer's hand
carved the turf
the soggy brown flesh
of the land
lies his uneyed skull
not singing

creep beneath the rock of memory
drift on our tide of dreams
and forget

that the summers were always
infused with sadness
the golden hours always
betrayed at birth
by memories of the future

follow our fingers to the gods
and hope they will not burn there
and now or never sing

rejoicing with the wind
in the chambers of our birth

Earth Man

I am an earth man –
Heather, gorse and grass
Are my jungle.
I grovel and revel
In the earth.
Sunlight flows through my fingers
Like water,
The sun brands me on anvils of stone.
I swim in the scents of flowers
And the sounds of bees.
I am radiant!
The sea fills my ears like shells
With the music of its moon-swayed mysteries.
I am enthralled.
The colours of light,
Of cloud and sky and rocks and trees,
Are daydreams screened before me.
Time turns, yes,
But slowly.
I taste heaven on earth.

Epitaph

Breathe softly, my love,
Raise not the storms that lurk
In the deep shadows of my soul,
Moist not your dry lips
On the autumn trees within,
Nor kiss my weathered heart;
Rest not your windswept arms
Upon my snowbound plains,
Where my memory – rails once shining
Desert-brown now and starving steel;
Nor touch not with your burning tongue
My icy brow to brand my brain
Yet more with brunt of blackness;
Oh yes, you are lightnings of darkness
In my already dark world,
Where I wander a night toy
With dark, dark blind hands;
Stir not, my love,
Upon my stillness, my coffined peace,
Where the spiders' webs even grind
A ghostly song around the twisted trees;
Speak not, my love,
Into the tomb of my mossy mouth,
To tremble there the sleeping spirits
And arouse time's dust-laden grin;
Place not your fingers coldholy
Upon my soilwarm face,
To trace the valleys of my tears;
Stir not the belfry where was my heart,
Where now blow through winds of silence –
Let us sleep still, I beg you,
Within our flowery grave.

eternity

eternity stalked time by the throat
clawed the life out of it
squeezed me out of it
tossed it back to the scavengers
to pick clean

i went quietly
my last moment blossomed and withered
all in the space of a lifetime

Faithful Departed

Our house stands in the shadow
Of the life that has left us –
The night is waiting patiently
To drift through our empty bodies:
It is lurking along the street
That died with the day's dying
And is scarred with the gashes
Of sunlight's downing;
The moon swims silently
Through the living room
And hangs in the mirror
Smiling at our sadness;
The room is now a dying room –
Death is creeping down the chimney,
Breathing down our necks too.

Fall

The autumn leaves are falling,
    As I am falling
    In love with you;
The autumn leaves are dying
    As I am dying
    With love for you;
The autumn leaves turn brown
    And tumble down,
    While I am blue
    For love of you.

False Faith

Reality has quick dissolved
    And down I plummet;
Worlds whirl, come and go of men
    And women clutching
    At green grass –

Legs have ridden, extracted
    Blind wild light from
This eternal coil of dark in my brain;
    Hands have prayed
But touched no clouds;
    Only monstrance was fat flesh
And fuse of far falling
    Selves, ever-membered meeting
Of bloody hearts, unrolling
    Of stones –

At midnight and beyond
    My continent of possession,
Chamber of a thousand years
    Swim and compacted nerve
All salved: a myriad miracles
    And vengeance for lost time
False faith,
    Glory to be –

Memory is no mantle:
    All is yet untouchable,
Irretrievable; but vision
    Blasted, blazed, and I
Sink my hand to the hilt,
    In sweet swirl of self.

Finale

1.

Only yesterday I stood on the grey stone bridge,
    Looking
At a green leaf waltzing giddily
    On its way
    To oblivion,
Alone with the deep sky and the deep water,
    Its ruptured nerves
Looking for the sun-fingered trees behind;
    A high and windy life I had of it
    And now I am afloat
    On these wintry waters
    Wasting

2.

It's cold and dark and I am silent
    Waiting
In an unknown follicle of the womb of life,
    And I am told
    That I am dead,
At least I've never been here before –
I feel the tender roots of grass growing
    Down into my clayface,
And in some great empty outside I hear
    Voices murmuring,
    The pattering of rain
And the noise of some awful machine coughing
    Laughing

3.

It's been a dark and wonderful day I think,
It's been a dark and wonderful life;
        I wonder if
        It's going to be as good,
        Now that
        I'm no longer living,
Now that I've been safely deposited for ever
        And for never;
There is only one slight disappointment –
        No more will I stand
        On the old grey bridge
And feel sorry for a dying leaf
        On the water
        In winter

4.

Now I must learn to be dead, the lesson of loss
        Deeper than death,
I must learn to sleep in darkness without
        My bedside lamp,
        My window of stars
        And long cool flow of the moon;
I must listen to the drumming of the rain
And the bugle of the wind
        Far and far above –
I must learn to live on the shadow side,
Beneath the softly beating soil, and I know now
        That this
Is the last and longest lesson
        Of them all

5.

In the darkness of my darkness I remember
        A vision of – love –
        Struggling
Through the farthest mists of memory,
        A flame to the ice of my heart,
        Burning away the coldness
        Into drops of blood.
I remember that I did not love. Perhaps then
        There is no hope now.
Paint my flesh with the blooded sword,
Anoint my eyes with perpetual darkness,
        Never let me live again
        On the frontiers of love

6.

The years have gone,
I'm still waiting, hoping that after life,
This is not simply the cruellest joke of all,
        That death does not exist,
        That I will have to die for ever
        In the twilight
        Of my guilt.
The voices have long gone and I wonder
        If it's spring.
 Then I see Him coming, stooping to look upon
        My ashes:
In His eyes I see the photograph of my guilt –
I gave you life and I gave you love, He says
        But you betrayed Me
        And you hated
And so He walked away leaving
The splinter of despair
        In my soul

7.

So this is the unfathomable mystery of death?
That I should be cast for ever solitary on the shores
   Of His hate,
Feel His blood that has flowed so freely,
   Drying an eternal pall
   Upon my breast?
How many years have passed now, I wonder –
   Ah, I had hoped that perhaps
Flowers at least would grow upon my grave,
That I could listen to them whispering,
   That they would talk to me,
   The most lonely corpse of all,
And laugh their pretty flower laughs and
   Even love me

.

flowers

a solitary flower in the suburban sunlight
knowing not the season
but fading all the same
bowing homage to the brown god –
will we plant tombstones on its grave?

the sun shakes her tresses of gold
down upon the city skyline
its chimneys like organ pipes
the city yawns and swallows the dawn
coughs and draws back the curtains
from its yellow teeth rises and
stubs out the magic night with
a crusty heel spits out the echoes
of the stars

the buses bustle officiously down
the meadows of flowers
cars yapping at their dusty heels
people have safely locked away their souls
crawl out with bleary minds
towards another evening
a clock signals the new lap smugly
another flower dies today

for each one of us

for each one of us
he strikes a match
in the darkness of the universe
but we always burn his fingers

Freedom Song

These birds have no wings,
They sing a song swift and high,
And blindly fly through the eyes
And through the hearts of gods and men,
Sprung from the fingers of ghosts
Who skulk behind faces of flesh,
Who will not recognise justice
Until it's spelt out in blood,
Until heads roll in their streets,
Their bombs tossed back at them;
They say they'd prefer peaceful means,
But their guns are not empty
And only their thoughts are blanks;
They complain they get no thanks
For guarding prejudice with thugs
And punctuating platitudes with slugs;
They are men who feed on fantasies
And cannot see their fallacies,
When the shadows begin to smother
The heart begins to beat violently
And the hand becomes a fist
Of indiscriminate self-defence;
All men are freedom fighters
With claws in their palms,
A final twist of the dagger,
A last spade of dirt on their breasts
And they will arise;
Fury is the final fling of defeat,
Which might turn it into victory;
Pride can lie low for years,
But will not die without a grab
At the throats of those
Who are trying to strangle it,
Their hands paralysed with power.

Funeral

The rain is beating on the coffin
The dull rhythm of the dead;
The black loam is sweet in the wet,
It swallows, swallows, swallows you
Into the rain-sodden voids of Golgotha;
Sink your fingers in and feel the darkness
Bulging through the ribbons of life;
Look at the damned wood that has to endure
Two shames and the shining brass
As it slides into the mystery;
There is no breath, there is no seed
And there is nothing new under the sun
Except the distant newness of geology;
Her blood and bones are meat to the soil –
There is no hope, only the end for ever.

Gone Girl

Your hair was fine
Spun cloud dark with
The din of rain
Your eyes held visions
Of lakegloom rank with
Dregs of stormsmell
Your lupinfragrant skin
Still shines like shell in
My deepsea diving memory
Your flesh was wheat
To the mills of my soul
Your hands that touched me in love
Were warm and wise as serpents

Hills

Hills huge with history hug the horizon,
Their birth a mystery in some soulless world
That hung in the heavens of a guilty god;
They are dumb and dark as fate itself,
Horror in their hearts at his unholy hand;
The fingers of fate have fashioned and framed them
For ever to be the symbols of our
Inscrutable destiny.

Eyes have held in their flickering flames,
As well as the fantasy of delightful death,
Their dreadful design, and dipped beneath
The shadows of their solemn shapes,
Their display of ultimate obscurity and fateful absurdity,
To see the savage print of their own
Uncertain and unascertained sentence,
Indefinite indemnity.

Sounding in the dimmest caverns of my mind,
The sea's sweet and suspicious sound,
Murmurings of mysterious memories,
Messages of ambiguous meaning
To the switchboard of my soul;
Ears have harvested soft sad music from the flood,
In awe I listen to the shells, to the sea's
Insubstantial story.

Earth and water encircle our necks,
Time-tied thus we dumbstruck,
With bulging hearts and lungs choked of life,
Are lowered softly from the levitation of our dreams;
We descend bewitched to the netherworld,
But moments have facets which must be turned
To collect the light of the star, ultrabeams of love, as
Dreaming we drown.

How Long

How long was I mistaken,
How long has it taken,
For me in the learning
That love is not a burning,
Nor a fancy in the eye,
Romantic pie in the sky;
That love is not for money,
It's not a pot of honey,
A gold or diamond ring
Or any physical thing –
No, to learn that love
Is something far above.

Holograph

City of stone and icy light,
Sky that sledges the buckled neck,
The brunt of being, bitter,
Wrung of life their feet in flight
Upon the backward flowing sea,
They grope for baptism of flesh,
Sweet fire that flares and flays,
Dance of flame-spirits in their thirsty eyes:
Love is their slake and their quick,
The blood-bond, graft of cell and weld of selves,
Cathedral to beyond within where …

horrorscope

the rose has fingered the thorn
and is bleeding
and the night is no longer perfumed
nor are there stars
to mourn its going or light
its darkened grave

and the moon is waiting deep
in darkness
for the sea to dawn upon
her rocky face
but the waters know not how
to rise again

and the earth is praying for
a new springtime
her bony hands beaded with
drops of ice
while birds build nests of sand
in the glass-edged wind

there is a hollow laughter
where the fountain
used to weep
and the pigeons are burrowing
beneath the concrete
fleeing for their lives

the people are ranked below
the townhall clock
crying to its handless face
and the maiden is bowed before
the newspaper stall
amazed with grief

for the rose has fingered the thorn
and is dying

If Only They Could See

If only they could see
All their dogmas and defences
Are walls in the hurricane
As flimsy as wafers
And we are all alone
So let's stay together
And be lonely no more
But find a little love
To shine against the dark
Before it encloses us.

I'll Never Fall in Love Again

I'll never fall in love again,
The water is too deep;
Secure on land I will remain,
And safe my feelings keep.

That was I thought my only wish,
Until I saw your face;
But now I've jumped in like a fish,
And sunk without a trace!

Imagination

The mind is not bound by earth or sky;
The electric invisible field of imagination
Is the medium of each moment,
From which it draws its sense of life,
A beam of glamour upon the inner screen,
Illuminating the pictures that besiege the eye,
In ceaseless conflict with the material monotony,
Its dramatic visions of an ideal world
Doomed to everlasting unrealisation.

In Glasnevin Cemetery

Gravestones, grief-engraved,
Pierce me to the soul;
The deaths of babies
Bring tears to my eyes;
The thought of *his* death
Chokes me like a noose:
His birth healed my heart –
His death would break it.

In John Donne's Time

They walked the world
Their arms whirled
Their pens were dipped
In blood and tears
Their legs carried them
Until they were folded
Laid away from the buffet of dreams
Straining for love in the face of death
Clutching for clouds while pinned to earth
Colossal they sighed and were seeded
With the earth where now we wander
Our feet on their foreheads
We too reach for the clouds
And falling back call for god
Falling back to earth

In The Human Scrapyard

Nature's treachery,
That makes you bow to the bond of love,
Then snatches the ring from your hand
And seals it beneath a stone;
While your knees do homage to Fate,
And the wind wrestles with your flowers,
Your heart swells to bursting,
Your cries boom around the universe,
Your tears spill like rain around –
The earth belches, bloated with
The fat of your sorrow.
The first barb is in your soul.
You feel the snake's fold around your throat,
That betrays you with a kiss.
When you lay your tattered roses
Upon the still stone, kiss it with your lips,
You feel then the tug of her spirit,
The gall of love breaks your heart.
You may walk blindly back to the ghosts
Or bury your heart there and then.

intergroove

a refined sadness
misery of life's mists in my bones
remind of lamplight kiss
beneath last night's scarved moon
whiskey glasses and tattle
music of stars prim with frost

drifts of past
banking up against
my fearful flesh

run deep the furrows of your joy
you will grow wilder
sink your heart in your blood
there are eternities swimming there
life and death coiled
heaven wed with hell
in a split second you're stretched
to breaking point
and beyond

have no truck with truth
engraved on tablets
or reality reaped in years
hold onto your dreams
they are older and younger
than you will ever be
shadows of unknown gods

Ireland

Roses in the rain,
Memories that bring
A mixture or emotions,
Pleasure mixed with pain.

Turf smoke, heather, pine,
Rain on a fresh breeze,
Smells as intoxicating
As any glass of wine.

The music's in my blood,
It rushes at the sound,
No symphony or song
Could ever be so good.

My history is whole,
When I read the tragic story,
It stirs up all my senses
And satisfies my soul.

jaguar

one flower in the suburban moonlight
houses held tight in the lips of night
shadows crawling vampire-like over graves
inside men stored for day of judgement
heads rolling through the future
tumbling from dream to dream
into the apron of a bloodshot dawn
tawny moon beached on our black roof
bracelets of light on the water
unknown god lolling in the lap of darkness
knees crossed aloofly reclining
on his cross made of moonbeams
with his crown of stars staring down
like a jaguar cat with pitiless eyes
waiting for the mice and men

Japanese Girl

With your glossy black hair
And black diamond eyes,
Your geisha-girl face
And lisping little-girl voice,
I fell in love with you,
Foolish old man that I am.

Oh, I didn't see the poison dart
That had pierced your pretty heart!

Your father didn't love you,
You told me with a tear or two;
Like a fool I said I'd take his place,
And you agreed to be my daughter;
But the poison was too strong,
Your heart was cold and dead.

Oh, I couldn't extract the poison dart,
That had pierced your pretty, lonely heart!

Or perhaps I'm just imagining it,
In order to deny the simple truth –
You couldn't love me because I'm old,
My hair is grey, my time has gone;
It was a stupid game to play,
I wish I'd never gone that way.

So now there's another poison dart
Inside *my* broken, bleeding heart!

kicking up the daisies

    the plane
spreadeagled on the sky
    silent as a spectre
shifts its sinister nose sunward
    and in a swerve of swift infinity
is sistered with the silken slumbers
    of the evensun

    my frail arms
tongue warm with pernod
    i wave
to the furrow of its memory
    in fond memory
of my childish dreams

    and turning upon
my heel to go am reminded
    by the chorus of worms
that i died two weeks ago
    died two weeks ago
ho ho ho hosanna ho

maybe now you will reject god
and all his works and pomps?

so the headworm downed his thumb
signalling my disinterment
and at my ardent objections
callously remarked
you have no sense of exhhumour
ho ho ho

Lacrimae Rerum

It makes me cry
To think one day
All love must die,
All dreams decay;
I wonder why
Life's made this way,
But neither I
Nor you can say.

Laden with Love

I'm laden with love,
Like fruit on a tree;
Just give me a shake
And it's yours for free.

I'm loaded with love,
Like honey on a bee;
Just give me a buzz
And I'll fly to thee.

How deep is my love,
As deep as the sea;
Just dive in the water
And be part of me.

Let Us Love

Like two rivers our lives have run into the same sea,
Like two birds our flights have crossed the same sky;
Time and space have coupled us, against incalculable odds,
And destiny made us lovers, so we must love our destiny;
Like two pieces of a cosmic jigsaw puzzle,
We bumped together and found we fit;
Let our limbs tie together in an unbreakable knot,
Weave into an imperishable tapestry
The threads of our dreams,
Make symphonies of the strings of our hearts,
Solder our souls in the heat of our love;
Let us remember that passion's friction
Is the only flame that warms our lives,
The only current that drives our blood,
The thunder and lightning in the dark
Of our empty skies, glimmer of heaven
In our desolate eyes. So let us love.

Letter to A Lost Lover

This is to let you know
That I love you first and foremost,
And that first and foremost
You will always be;
But also to let you know
That you must let me be free,
You must always let me go
Wherever my spirit entices me;
If you cannot understand
You must find it in you to agree –
You will if you love me as I love you,
That is, to the last degree;
My love for you is endless
And perfect like a circle,
But you mustn't try to encircle me;
So remember, you are first and foremost
And will always be,
But I am free.

Life

Life is not a bed of roses,
That's what my father rails;
He's wiser than he supposes —
It's a bed of bleedin' nails!

Life Is Just a Dream

Doesn't it sometimes seem
That life is just a dream,
That when we die,
We'll give a cry
Of delighted surprise,
Waking up in Paradise,
Or maybe a yell,
If it's in Hell,
Look back at this phase
As a kind of daze?

On the other hand,
Maybe death's a land
Of everlasting night,
Without a gleam of light,
A sort of unconscious lake
From which we'll never wake
Our bearings to take:
To gaze at the stars,
Or contemplate Mars,
And indulge in the ponder,
Is there anything yonder,
Or despondently quiz,
Is this all that there is?

Long Wave

I reach out my hands and feel sounds,
The beating of a tree's heart,
The music at the centre of a stone,
Prehistoric pulses in my palms;
I shut my eyes and hear waterfalls
In the cave of my cranium,
Tides of unconceived words,
Topple and flood of pictures
In my blood.

I have reached the horizon,
I am adrift in inner space,
Swallowed into the uterus,
Beyond the whirl of words or wands,
Beyond all galaxies of known dreams,
Beyond the voice and vision of friends,
I am alone.

At the extremes of life and death,
My cells are billions of light years away,
Stars on the borders of my memory;
They fade and I remain suspended
In the plasma of selfhood –
Tortured echo of the demon's voice,
Terror of ghostly visions flitting
Across the distant screen of my mind,
They see me in this fractured mirror
And call me crazy.

I am a spaceship in the galaxy of my thoughts,
Locked in the spin of self-invasion,
Beyond the circumference of time
And trap of tradition;
I am the light in a leaf,
The flutter of light on the water,
The sway of the pine tree in the clouds,
And the ripple of the wind on the water too;
I shut my eyes and hear waterfalls
In the cave of my cranium,
Tides of unconceived words,
Topple and flood of pictures
In my blood.

Lost in Space

The sound of a woman's grieving
Vibes through the evening stillness
Into my consciousness,
Until my mind is sagging
Beneath the weight of it;
It's the shell of love's language,
Arising from the infinite spaces
Of her blacked-out, starless soul.

Broken by the strain of everyday living
And everyday dying she weeps –
It's the soil's very blood,
Ichor of sadness;
The woman has felt the pulse of death
With her grief-contorted hands,
Hands that had loved and loved so well.
Now they are unloving, unloved, adrift,
Lost in space.

Lost Girl

No words can chart
The tides of dread
That sway her heart
And swirl inside her head.

Loughduff

It was evening
As I walked along the rosy shore
     Of the setting sun
And listened to the shellborn sealight;
The pines were ragged
     In the water
     Blowing through them
     Down the green folds,
And around the lake clouds of heather-haze
Tangled with the music of evening bees –
     Twilight zither
     And hayfumes
     Upon the day's going.

My eyes were shells to the ear
     Of the setting sun,
And I could see all the world fallen back,
     Leaving nothing but the earth,
     Reeds bowing in the breeze
     Above the lake, coldly fishjealous
     Sentinels.

And along the disused railway travel of silence,
     Rabbits sprung with fright,
     And the signal post a spectral finger;
And I dipped my hands in the lake-laden wind,
     Sails in the green ways
     Blowing down the trees
     And I felt free.

loughside

a wet green summer afternoon
  in deepest County Cavan
my feet fixed on the shingle bed
  of the Derries loughs
ankle-deep in swirling sky
  away at the soothing centre
far away from the spin of the world
  cracked and scratched blarer
idle flowers cistercians trees
  green grass flowing along the shore
asperges of wind and water
  swells of grey cloud hustling up
from the rushes
  a swelter of silence
extracting the essence of my thoughts
  below the rim of the world
that wants to box and pummel me
  but the swift winds have picked
the fibres from my clogged flesh
  swept the cobwebs from my eyes
the rainbow trout just like my thoughts
  sliding over brown and pink pebbles
a boat's rotten carcass ribboned with moss
  for me to breathe
the wind shoots reels of light
  across the lake
flurries of silver through the green
  i float away
the piano strings of memory vibrate
  to this intimation
of eternity

.

Love Grows

Lust is a feeling that comes and goes,
Love is one that grows and grows;
Ah, but the years, they come and go,
And love, I'm afraid, doesn't always grow.

love poem

so you broke above the mountains
of my melancholy and hung aloft
bird of prey sexy darling
come hunting for my heart it's yours
can i help it if you dawned
at midnight dispelling me?

love poem on a tightrope

unparched sprouting to the sky
like a tree of summer is borne
our love and fruits of this
ascendant of our souls a vain
and fragile wanting soft tendril rooted
in mortality

and yet decant hope unsubservient
breathing in the essense of our lives
does it not transform become a thing
of joy seem to visit from some outer
dark of which our souls have but
fleeting memories

element yes my mind's ambuscades
prefabricated tell i to be for
this fragrance i suspect is
deeper rarer still a thing thriving
in my outer senses which may not even
be senses

but the borders of the greater life
to which i append which could i troth
be called god – no matter i may take
my finger from such a heart and look
only to the wild winds and sunsets
in your eyes

for the joy remains inviolate and
let all else die away from me it is there
a sacred presence which i would quail
to repudiate which i embrace which
in spite of life's corruptions i will keep
deep chambered in my heart

you may not even know this genesis
and me a pilgrim in my desert dreams
mocked and yet i will harbour even them
for i sense that dreams such as these
are ambassadors of heaven come
for my redemption

howsoever it is here i cast my life
to this bourne i wend and here will garner
truth that joy which is a fugitive of words
that you are and will ever have been
with me as cold as ice
a silver axe down the centre
of my tomb

Love's Treachery

I think it's better that we part,
Each try to make a brand new start;
I tried in vain to let you see
Through the veil to the inner me,
But when you did, you fell apart,
And now you nurse a broken heart.

I loved you deep, as deep could be,
Far deeper than the deepest sea,
But for such seas you had no chart,
So now you've gone to live apart;
I never thought *you* could ever be
Capable of such a treachery –
It's left another poisoned dart
Inside my broken, bleeding heart.

Lullaby

The moon shines on the child's face
Beguiling him into a land
Of dreams and fairytales;
Now his young mind is clothed in sleep
Adrift in the treetops and skies
Of his diaphanous imaginings;
Let the night play to him
Its overtures of happiness,
Its fluting hollow melodies,
For there is little else left
Once the night has gone.

market street apocalypse

this afternoon
has woven in me
a new strand of sympathy
brought to my narrow lips
a communion at once
more bitter more sweet
than wine and bread
communion of true flesh and blood
which it saddened me to see
with its attendant woes
so many of those people suffering
as they shuffled past
and beyond me
sometimes even smiling
and i passed them wondering
at their desperate constancy
dispensing secretly
some of the pity i had reserved
for myself yes pity
whose seed i'm sure is love
even in my own case
and secretly i wished them well
grateful to have been touched
by their presence
i who am something of a fatalist
and as i paused to buy a newspaper
reflecting on the human spirit
which can endure these things
i prayed fervently
that there might be ahead
for all of us
a better life
if not a better death

memento

when the wheel of life
  turns my mind to shadows
and i move in leaf-tossed rain
  upon brown mould
my eyes fly to that vision
  enshrined within my soul
that echo of music in the hall
  flash of gold in grey
transcending mere memory
  which brushes the window-pane
of my haunted heart
  makes bouldered streams tumble
in the clefts of my arid soul
  warm blood to spring
to the cliffs
  of my cobbled bones

when i remember her smiling eyes
  the petals alight upon
the plain of time between us now
  settling in the dust of my dreams
like confetti on a sepulchre
  a melodious light sounds faintly
deep in the valleys of my eyes

Memories

Time is whispering through the grass
Shining like hair in the sunlight;
Forgotten years stumble out of haybarns
And buried faces stare from the tiger-lilies;
A lifetime has settled quietly on the fields
And there are voices in the rusty leaves
Dying in the autumn orange splendour;
The silken robes of dawn unfold
Their cool emotions into a warm memory
And there is left a wispy sadness
Curling through the sun-twisted trees,
Where my feet can never travel more;
The mind can feel the feeble pulse of death
And listen to the heart-deep mysteries
At the centre of things, lives of people
Loved and forgotten for ever lost –
For people will love and forget
Our broken little lives too.

metaphysical jerks

so the worst is out
our tongues have sought to trace
the mystery of life
the mystery of everyday death

but our tongues write in sand
our fingertips are only
the beginning of the end

the girl in white
on the grass plain
has the moon and stars at her feet
but her feet are feet of clay
haceldama of the heart

oh why is it not the other way round?

the fuses are all blowing
we will all blow unless
we keep our heads firmly in the clouds

walking on walls of flesh
the walls of death
my soul is in her hands
the precipice to which she clings

Micro

The grass grows and bends,
    And browns to the braying winds,
    And in the baby's blood flow
Grains of grit, and seeds of a strange soul.

The stars shine and wheel,
    And wince in the rocket's roar,
    And in the child's soul spring wondrous
Blooms of light, and broods of insect fears.

The man grows and shines,
    And claps his hands to his gods,
    But in his eyes are grains of sand,
And in his heart the nerves are whispering.

The years unspool and roll,
    Weave a wavering web,
    Clouds unravel, stars fall,
And on the man's lips the earth turns to cinder.

The sky shakes and falls,
    And brings the whelm of weird,
    Roof of time to floor him,
A shroud of sorrow, slab of stone to doom on him.

Mystic Miry

Looking for the first time
Into your lovely eyes,
I felt a joyous memory
Of some forgotten paradise;
So I really start to wonder
If perhaps it could be true,
We met in some mystic yonder,
Miry, me and you?

My reason tells me nonsense,
It's just a romantic notion,
And yet it seems mysterious,
As the deepest, darkest ocean,
That though we only had a week
Of kisses, words and beers,
I feel as if I've known you
A hundred thousand years.

nightmare

the moon-flooded sea
 slides black and silver through
my hurricane eyes:
 sly gulls with shingle
in their throats
 hurtle through
my boiling brain and
 pick my dreams trailing
them all colours of the rainbow
 crystals of heaven upon
my jetsam: the waves are
 frilled with dawn and
snarl with teeth of glass
 in the face of my ghost:
his mouth is like a god's
 swallows all things eats up
the world and licks the ichor
 from lips of wool:
i gambol in the company
 of ghosts play sticks
with my bones scream up
 the deepest hell bury
my soul in the sand and look
 with glass eyes on what has now
turned to lead:
 i raise my feeble fist in
the beak of the storm
 belch thunder and strike
lightning from my flinty heart:
 the storm slices off my head
and i watch my white blood
 bubbling in my strands
i cut my wrists on the moon
 and am enrolled in
the company of men

nights in black satin

then the nights
took me with sorrow
clutched and rattled me
hard-billed metaphysical witches
and all by the light of

a silvery moon
shining through skeletal towers
turning the wood to bone
scattering the shoulders of meadow
with seas of glass

drawing tears deep down
from the most tender roots
and hurling them
to unlistening roofs
wrecking me

nocturne

the virgin moon
spreads her sea-cape
upon the silent world
she dreams

the wind weaves
webs of gossamer-music
through the poplars
voices beckon
her unharboured mind afloat
the moon conducts her boat
into the garden of dreams

blowing kisses to the sky
and surpliced with starlight
she dances a suite of shadows
swansweet grace the circles of
her unsubstanced soul
she slips into the streams
of her joy

but morning
a river of tears will run
when to meet her
still of day and break of brain
and dawn will wash her ghost upon
the planks of this world
flotsam of the fluid
of eternity

her dreams unpurled
weeds of noon to be
her wrestling-place
rosaries of sand
her fingers toll

Not Even She

Not even she, and how could I expect it,
Can understand
How deep I have sunk, how high I must fly,
The deathly land,
Nor the stratosphere of my spirit now,
The skeletal hand,
The devils and angels that play in my heart,
Extraterrestrial command,
The fact that I'm different and changeable
As sand,
Must follow a flight
Alone, out of sight,
Of dreadful delight,
Beyond all rhyme and reason,
Though she calls it treason,
To a star in my mind
Whose light outshines love.

Oh God

Oh God, set the night adrift,
Because there are days which should not be
In Your world!
Were you sad the day you invented Death,
The day you invented being and the subtraction of being?
The day You invented Your greatest glory
And Your greatest tragedy?
You made Heaven and Hell,
You made night and day,
You made life and death –
You made and unmade Yourself!

On A Lover's Suicide

Midnight sky streeling above my head,
Shaking from its tumbling clouds
Acid raindrops to mingle with
The burning tears upon my face;
She went laughing out of my life,
Reaching out with ecstasy
For annihilation and annihilation of our love;
Now the stone stands over the grave,
An everlasting monument to her triumph;
The warm green grass curls around her
A curtain of eternity to my world;
Somewhere in the air lingers the sound
Of her lost voice, as mysterious as music;
Somewhere in the groping greedy land
Lies her flaxen smile and cascading eyes;
I have my memory, but memory is a beach
And a tide of sorrow is coming in.

On the Death of a Fifteen-Year-Old Boy

Hearing that he was dead
Was like a hammer blow on *my* head –
The shock travelled down my spine
Into the very pit of my belly,
Filling my guts with dread
That one day I too would be dead;
The car fell on his head:
It must have been instantaneous
The doctor said –
He never even bled!
And yet, he was dead ...

Poem in a Nutshell

Through the web of the world's woe,
We are designed to go;
To sail on silver seas
We imagine our destiny to be –
But it's through the web of the world's woe,
We are designed to go.

Railway Lines

A bleary day towards the end of September,
One of my twelve favourite months,
And there is no sun, only cloud;
I stand below this creamy parchment sea
Of anonymity, within this railway tract,
On top of this people-less country,
Looking down the line wondering
Where everything comes from,
Where everything goes?
The telegraph lines with birds,
Like notes of music, crotchets and quavers,
Sitting pretty, spurning evocation,
Dismissal or even contemplation,
Black beaky little balls of fluff,
Trying to decide between
Africa or Southend for the weekend.

A sudden woosh and zoom
And they are plucked aloft
By invisible silken strings,
Exploded into fluttery flight,
So many feathers with life aquiver.
What happens to a bird when it dies
In mid-flight anyway?
It knows better than to look for heaven
Up there I'm sure!
Perhaps it becomes a cloudlet
Or a grain of sunlight –
Why not since it may already be
An iridescent starling?

A plume of smoke doffs the scene –
Cha cha cha, cha cha cha, the faceless engine
Hauling itself hugely along, bloated and belching,
In all its mechanical pomp and circumstance,
Silver shanks sulsing in and out, in and out,
Insensate dinosaur creeping by,
Sniffing wheezing grunting groaning
Prehistorically dumb – hoo hoo hoo –
What happens if *this* should die in mid-flight?
Then I *would* have a sleeping beauty on my hands!

Reduction Ad Absurdum

Flame of fortune on bare bone burning,
Upon a whirlpool of fire dancing,
Life's fast and furious waters,
Swirl of hell-gas and rattle of stone
In the guts. The angels' wings are plucked,
Heart has shrivelled to jaundiced sac,
Bled on the scathe of earth's rim.
Full fingers scooped up grace and
Wove tapestries of the future past – and now
There are haggard hands around the throat,
Serpent shadows and time's teeth in the pit;
The mystery of the universe circles stealthily
Around each newborn. The stars in their eyes
Are dagger-points of eternity and unknown end;
Meanwhile the maggots turn, fretful tug of time,
Elastic darkness wrings the soul,
Savage gravity of death.

reflections

black coals in their red skins
smoking along the fenceway
and the tracts of wasteland
from which float willow-herb
to sail in the September sunlight
while i pause to consider
my out of placeness

high over there in the sky-slit
a sharp finger of jet
which phantom-like Olympian-like
an unanchored tangent scissored
from its hypotenuse shoots
unseen trigonometries of runways
and is loose in the sky
an aluminium pterodactyl
fusion of prehistory with future
symbol of ambiguity of time

summery road bright with blossom
clouds of green rising from earth
Cheshireland greenrobed and cushioned
curled oblivious warm and beautiful
like a napping cat upon the grey
the grey grey carpet of road

road that has been here
in and out of the village of Didsbury
since medieval times when the Mersey
was a wild torrent and not now as if
diffident of its riverhood a very shy river
an unassuming river unless provoked
a river like the donkey that has had its day

but instead of becoming one with all this
we whizzed through car-bound
and the wonder of immobility occurred to me
because such moments are like
holes in the sails of time
taking time by the horns
and thrusting through its clavicles
the sword of at least our temporary immortality
though we can never hope to touch
its black, black heart

no suicide is not the answer
that would only be presenting the oblation
before its time

refugee

set adrift on the world
sailing from the familiar shore
of love and knowledge and belief
tattered sails of my visions
rotted shrouds of my prophecies
from the landslide of my illusions
i wing into wilderness

the wastelands behind
are stabbed with the crosses
of my dead idols
my eyes flee back
for some sign of life
some seed of sound
to stir the barren limbs
but i ride on

at least i have the armour of light
and yet i miss the old country
the torrid darknesses
jungles of dark music
where white doves prowled
the swales and sweeps of salvation
the valley and folds of folly
the mild grey shadow of purgatory
where every mountain pointed to Hell
and the stars were Heaven's footlights

but now i've cast my seeds
upon stony skies
now i have blinding light in my eyes
a monody of freedom in my brain
the peril of flight in my bones
and i am uncrucified

Requiem for My Father

The body was buried
In a box of beech and brass,
Obscenely beautiful,
In a field of ragged grass;
It was a sleet December day,
As they shovelled on the clay.

Seeing him lying on his bed,
I could not believe it true,
That *my* dad was really dead –
But his fingertips were blue,
And not a single puff of breath
Was the surest sign of death.

It's hard to comprehend
What was yesterday a man,
Was once a babe in arms,
Is today a piece of trash;
It makes it all so meaningless,
All the struggle, strain and stress.

There is no consolation,
Except fantasy and myth,
No verbal combination,
That can tell the truth of death;
We all go the same sordid way –
There's nothing we can do or say.

The body was buried
In a box of beech and brass,
Obscenely beautiful,
In a field of ragged grass;
It was a sleet December day,
As they shovelled on the clay.

Riding to Mass

Riding to the chapel
Through the dewy morning air,
Smells of new-mown hay and heather,
Of turf smoke, grass and pine,
Fill my lungs like ether.

The country lanes whir beneath my wheels
Empty and mysteriously silent, except for
The chirping of some early birds,
The lowing of invisible cows in misty meadows,
And the occasional donkey's bray
That leaves the silence
Even more mysterious than before.

Across the bog I rattle,
Picking my way carefully,
Over the brown springy earth,
Between the holes of black stagnant water
Like the evil eyes of hell;
I ride my rusty, rattling bike,
Breathing in the odours of the day –
Like incense they fill my soul;
Speeding down the hill
To Mullahoran chapel,
I'm laughing, I'm singing hymns,
I'm on a high, I'm on a roll,
I'm riding high to Heaven.

Rock-a-Bye Baby

From the mystery of the midnight hour
Come my thoughts wrapped in twisted dreams –
My child is there on the bed,
Like all children born of darkness,
With darkness circling to reclaim him;
The smile of the rogue has gone,
Fled to the core of his being
Leaving only a tattered remnant of joy;
Oh God, why are you so greedy
For our happiness?

Sea Bird

You are a creature born
Of earth and sky,
Upon the wind you sail,
Seas of the world
Reflected in your eye,
Your wings riding waves of light
While on and on you fly.

Upon the shore we stand,
We watch and gasp with awe,
We cannot see the things you see,
We know no port but land.

Simon [R.I.P. Nov. 2008]

Simon, you sad, silly man,
We were your friends,
Though you didn't know it,
But nor did we.

Perhaps we should have told you,
Perhaps you should have asked,
But we were silent,
Busy with ourselves.

Besides you seemed OK,
Or were you just pretending?
Well, so were we,
Pretending all was well.

We should have broken down your door,
Before the boys in blue!
We should have smashed through the glass,
The pane you hid your pain behind.

But regrets are of no avail,
Let's hope you're somewhere better;
At least we have good memories,
And not a word of scorn for you.

You left too soon, you had more to give,
The world is worse without you;
But your spirit lives on among us,
The gifts you gave, the light you shone.

Thank you, Simon, and farewell,
Until and if we meet again;
We always will remember you,
The man we never really knew.

Remember us if you can,
And shine a light down here;
Yes, we will remember you,
You sad, sweet, silly man!

(I've used the word 'silly' here mainly in its old Anglo-Saxon meanings of
'blessed', 'happy', 'innocent'... Simon was a colleague of mine who sadly
took his own life.)

Sleep, Little Baby

Sleep, little baby,
Do not fear,
For while you sleep,
Your daddy's near;
Don't worry, I won't tell
Of my secret fear,
Which is, I'm afraid,
I won't always be here.

Snow

You are a tide of snow
Beating on the burning shores
Of my battered heart;
You are the candle in the window
On my dark night of the soul;
I would pluck out my eyes to see you,
Cast away my hands to touch you,
Cut out my heart to love you!
Our fires will become an inferno,
Our songs a symphony of love;
Together we can reach the stars,
Fly to infinity and beyond;
I look at your hair and see
Fields of fallen leaves,
I look at your face and see
Gardens of angelic flowers,
I look into your eyes
And believe in god again!
Your hands are tablets of stone
On which I read my destiny,
When you lay them upon me
I die and go to heaven;
Your lips are like the doors of ecstasy –
When you kiss me I'm born again,
A celestial light bursts through my brain;
Let's walk hand in hand into the darkness
And die upon this midnight mood
Of love beyond over and above.

Squib

In spite of all the religious prattle,
Life I'm sure is a losing battle;
Where we come from there is no knowing,
Nor the answer to where we're going.

subsidence

the season after winter
and before spring
when the snow has slipped
to scape of still
when the seas press you down
among things unknown
the clouds with gentle smiles
pin you to the cushion of earth

when the trees bow
to fan your empty head
with memories
before turning away
when snow turns to stone
and the world sighing
hurries home

everlasting waves of stillness
flakes of silence
heap around your head

cold and wild and lost
the rain hurtles through
your barns of illusion
the ground plucks your bones
of all the red hot flesh
winds pluck your eyes

all things move away from me
nursed to perfect tranquillity
you sigh and settle in
the cradle of the shell
ocean pillow afloat on the dark
the mighty one bears you silently
around and around and around

Suicide

He walked one summer's morning
Down to the river and the reeds,
Went under the water,
Under the world's skin
That shone like silver;
The ducks squabbled and
A breeze made the reeds waltz.

All his life he had worn
A halter about his neck;
He talked and laughed and seemed glad,
But his head was a chamber of horror,
His heart got colder and colder;
His eyes had to see beneath the skin,
His ears had to hear the earth's heartbeats,
Which broke like hammers
In the hold of his own
Broken heart.

The stars' strains, the blood on the rose,
The music of his fears was maddening;
The world's laughter was stretched
Like a thong around his mind
And tears – a tide that swept him
Over the brink of his endless
Receding sanity.

Tales

The tales they tell,
The knots they tie,
Their souls to sell,
It makes me cry;
Their talk of Hell
And Heaven high,
I know full well
Is all a lie.

thanksgiving

walking upon the poachy loughside
  in the early morning wind
as it flows emerald and scented
  of water still silent as
the deepest night which now it has shed
  from coolest skies and pastelled
with faint sunrise coming upon me
  i pause to think
to have thought of you then
  would have been purest heaven
and ascension of my soul –
  for which unborn music i pray now
    to your angel's hands

that girl's dreams

that girl's dreams
all revolve around
an infant star
a tenderness in the deep
of night
i hope will rise
and anoint her soul
with chrism of green
her eyes with oil of rose
echoes of eternity
blind vision for
her spaceless arms

the existentialist

i have thrown brazenly and temariously
the garbage of my existence to the dogs
i have stepped out of today and yesterday
out of the mountains and the sea
gone forth from mankind
and the cushions of brick and concrete
where my soul has hitherto nestled
these many moons
where my nerves have bathed
these many snows

and now i breathe in the dark
feel my lungs swell with dark
and the dark explodes inside my eyes
and i drown in the dissolution

there is no perimeter to this destruction
no penumbra of infinity
the finger of fate cracks and flees
and god curls up within his shell
oblivious and disgusted

my soul rises weightless
to hover the expanse of her loneliness
no talons to grip
dialogue of none
tongue swept away on waves of thought
cogito ergo non sum
eyes swept away on brainwaves

i am reduced to the ultimate
the molecule wherein i begin and end
and yet still am not nor am
nor taste of ash nor fruits of paradise
nor absence of darkness
no abraham to plunge in the truth
and divide me for ever into
everlasting truth
mushrooms not growing outside of death
yielding release from bondage of being

The Key

Let me give you a kiss
And tell you this:
This love of yours
Has opened doors
To the innermost part
Of my mysterious heart,
And there I've discovered,
Or rather, recovered,
A feeling of bliss
I've so long missed;
I hope that you'll stay
And love me this way,
Through joy and through tears,
For the rest of our years;
Please stay in my heart,
Of which you're a part,
And as for the key –
Let it drop in the sea!

The Light of Love

The light of love,
Like a candle in the wind,
Can be lost in the hurricanes of life.
It is so frail, sometimes flickers
And almost fails.
Don't let it die.
It's a sacred flame
A divine luminance.
The star that warms and lights
The bleak voyage of our lives
From oblivion to oblivion.
Don't let it die.

The Old Rustic Bridge by the Mill

The impetuous river
Races over the rocks,
Raking the moss
Into green tresses;
The wind capers
Through the budding trees,
The sun sparkles and glitters
On the mercurial water;
Cows silently chew the cud
In velvet-green fields,
While cottages slumber,
Puffing turf smoke like incense;
A pheasant leaps
From the long bracken
Into the mystic silence
With a clatter of wings
And takes to flight –
Then silence falls again,
Except for the rush of the river
Over the ragged rocks
And around the ruins of the mill,
Eroding them, insidiously,
Like time the mill of my heart.

the passing of love

those that the passing of love
takes by surprise are they
who have felt heaven on earth
but are now drowned in hell
numb sorrow white as bone
throat of all agony
splinters of memory
in their skinned souls
who have been launched
deep down in the depths of being
above the above
beyond all words, all stars ...

when flesh is god to flesh
and in one communion are
a thousand million eternities
but the pendulum swings
the world spins faster faster
time's sour grin swallows all
the mad whirl of molecules
allows no quiescence
no unanchored mind
no sway of everlasting soul

The Sovereign Moon

The sovereign moon shines pitiless
On the swirling seas of my life;
Every autumn a leaf of my life falls
And every spring my heart rises again;
I'm a nomad between birth and death
Seeking a star that will shine
With a luminance more divine
Than the simple gift of breath;
Love is a morning star
But it has its evening too,
Darkness will lay its hand
On my eyes to make me blind
One time through all eternity,
Strike me dumb and deaf,
Draw a blind across my mind;
And now while I live this life
I must live with a lunatic joy,
Do all that my heart commands;
On the peak I must laugh and dance
Beneath all men, above all gods,
Alone in my redemption
Upon my cross of self,
Without understanding or defence.

time

at the centre
of every circle
another
at the heart of every flower
another
at the end of every other
beginning without end
out of sight
out of mind
a point sharpened
to invisibility
silver chain
sparkle of diamond
in the bowels
of the abyss
neck of hour-glass
uncircumscribable
sterile grains
of our eternity
sands of time
crumbled between
our fingers

Time and Time Again

I am rocked between past and future,
My vision is a vice, stereoscopic;
Around the borders of my brain
The ghosts of future days dance darkly;
In the twilit mirrors of my mind
The fiddles weave warped symphonies
That compress my panic-panting heart
To a standstill –
The locomotive clangs through
The platform of my mind,
I do not move, I fear
The sunlight is a web,
A fantasy resurrection
Of yet unborn epiphanies,
Recalled by some imaginary eye
In the spin,
Within the ever-whirling,
Ever-rolling, ever-reeling
Gyromancy of time.

Time Being

Beauty is like light
Flowing in a circle
Eyes must be swift
Mind like mercury
To scoop in the flash;
We should shoot our dreams
The cataracts of each eternal moment,
Before the rivers run
From whence they came
And we are back to earth again –
The roaring night will not stay
That sweeps us on our way.

to be

to cleave yesterday
from my life
to scour the scum
of so many vain emotions
and fix my eyes my hands
upon tomorrow now

to escape from time and mutability
outwards inwards and around
the confines of cloud and worm
sail from the point of the pine tree
from this galaxy of dates

leaving grandfather sun
to hobble to his doom

and thus dismantled
be
is
am

To My Unborn Son

From dizzy dreams
To depths of despair,
Life has swung me;
Round and round we go
In ever smaller circles
Like a needle round a record
Until the music stops,
The dance is done,
Our hearts like worn-out metronomes
Our lives like broken clocks;
Yet the earth spins on,
Sun rises, sun sets …
It's yours, my son,
With my regrets,
I will not be able to save you
From the dance's final steps;
How I wish it could be different,
That in giving you birth
I could promise you heaven
On this godforsaken earth –
But you decide its worth;
All I can give is love,
But love to life
Is like a heart
Against a knife,
A flame against
A glacier of ice,
No match against
The deadly loaded dice.

travelling snowman

upon the train
shooting through the setting sun
and the swinging gull
upon the unsprung earth

we go

collecting anemones for
our unmade graves
from the altars of
experience

we die before our time

gowned in clay
the sun our diadem
we dance towards
our destiny

we go

with posterity
yapping at our heels
that burn the dust
and lulled we lie

we grin

at the snow thawing
on our fingertips

and meekly melt away

Tumbling Dice

My love is cold and clear,
My love's as hard as ice;
I impose no conditions,
I don't exact a price;
I love you without fear,
I take the tumble of the dice.

tunnelling

vagrant dreams where I tunnel
in my asbestos boots
hands trace dark-slimed walls
new heart spored by darkness
scope of light at end

i pluck out and cast away
the glass eye of intellect
parachute into the night
suspended by my nerves
vertigo
knowing that truth
has to be ploughed for
is sown in sweat
and blood and years
reaped in mystery
untasted forbidden fruit

blood is purified by mystery
through heart fleeced of faith
soul bathed in spring of hope anew
one atom of humility
is worth a thousand frontiers
of knowledge
i dedicate myself
to the unknown
i lay my life down there
to the clap of thunder
and shuddering storm

Two Girls

Two girls in pink pullovers,
Both beautiful, sound as a bell;
It just goes to show,
You never can tell!

Unfinished Symphony to Lydie

You've sent out vibrations
Which have touched the aerial of my soul,
Crossed the infinite distance between us
And entered the nucleus of my being,
Splitting the atom of my ego
Into a million particles,
Which form now in my soul
A rainbow in the raindrops of your love.

You have opened a chamber in my heart
Which was shut, empty, silent,
Waiting for you.
You're there now
And I've thrown away the key.

My heart wants you as its guest for ever,
I hope you'll stay;
You've penetrated the womb of my being,
You're like a foetus now,
Growing inside me, growing, glowing,
Lover beloved.

Like a spaceship from afar
You've travelled into my universe
And I into yours,
So let's stay for ever in orbit
Around each other.

Upon Being Born

The beginning of the brightness
Was in flesh,
Where I saw the living caverns of love,
But touched not their warm walls,
Nor did my astronaut eyes travel
Through their carnal skies dawnfed;
And yet it was their nighthissing pistons
That drove me into the spaces,
My creeping limbs.

But the beginning of the beginning
Was in stone,
The valley of some god's fecund beauty,
Some glacial stillness carved
From the furthest rocks of time,
Fissured with the foetus-blood of stars;
And there my hands were bedded beyond day
Until their birth in night
To grow old.

I was a seed of mystery aloft in darkness,
My soul enshrined in eternal being
And clothed with victory,
To be worshipped by the unmade moon;
I was invisible,
A nerve in the mind of some black pre-dawn sun,
I was all and nothing,
I was.

Venice

No moon, no stars, no breezes blow,
No sun, no rain, I'm feeling low;
A city slips beneath the sea,
My lover has deserted me.

My heart is like a haunted place,
Haunted by her ghostly face;
I wish I knew some spell or prayer,
To make her fade away from there.

There is no God, there cannot be,
To inflict this pain on such as me;
She was my way, my truth, my light,
I'm like a man who's lost his sight.

It happened there, in St Mark's Square –
The photo shows her standing there –
'I don't love you,' she said to me,
As the city slipped beneath the sea.

walk the line

the train rolls
down the line
but the centre of the circle
is *my* destination
walking on the tracks
ladders of my dreams
i tread upon a summer's day
wish i was going somewhere
instead of dreaming dreams
sinister silence surrounds me
so i kneel on the shale
and put my ear to the rail
to listen to the tune
like some magic music
from faraway lands
a foretaste of the future
vibrating through my lonely heart

War Symmetry

Those men were babies once,
Now buried like dogs' bones,
Sweepings of butchers' shops,
Crosses like macabre crops.

But we face the same fate,
With death we have a date;
Maybe they're the lucky sods,
Already gone to meet their gods.

Waterfall

Like dynamite you detonated
The dam of my love,
And swept me away
On the ensuing flood.

No arrow ever flew
So fast or true,
As the shaft of my love
When I first met you;
No river could glide
So deep or wide,
As the flood of my love
Encompassing you.

We're born, we die,
No reason why;
We begin, we end,
It's a fact we can't mend.

You don't believe in words,
But my words I send like birds
Into the skies of your eyes;
Nor do you believe in tears,
But my tears I send and fears
Over the weirs of your ears.

Downriver we float,
In life's fragile boat,
Till over we fall
Death's waterfall ...

When Love Fled

When love fled,
Our hearts bled;
When love died,
Rivers we cried –
Tears and blood,
A sorrowful flood;
For our dreams we wept,
As away they swept,
For our hopes we bled,
As away they sped;
But blood and tears
One day will have dried,
And despite our fears,
We will have survived.

wild ghosts

empty-handed travellers
pilgrims trapped between life and death
flowers springing from their hearts
to wilt in the darkness of their breasts
they sow and spin catch at rainbow dreams
see visions and die

strings of lights pole to pole
across the arctic wastes of their minds
lead them lurching blindly on
boxed in by past and future
rocks rolling crack of doom
on doomsday daily

finding themselves deceived
that the universe seems but a hole
in God's brain they cry for blood
to irrigate the arid plains of history
and they pounce on their prophets
sink rabid fangs into their hearts

who can blame them
their memories are always born
premature still as stars
and twice as far away

windy night

baroque sky scrolled with cloud
where curl and weave and spin sparrows
undrainpiped unbricked unhoused unhedged
swinging seagulls upon the zephyrs
gaunt beauties aswoop above the ground
where the trees flither in the wind
tidal with green and shadow of green
to and frother and alow the sandy sky
sings the wind southerly a psalter
susurrant choir of surpliced trees
coultered sky dimming now neath
the sisping night whisp-bird aflute
to trail the broiders of the dark
fadered now unfeathered
trees yawling wind-weary for a lullaby
to lull their linden-limbs
and repose in peace colombial
unshackled spockled speckled
dabbered shafts of grunging night
buckling all down and basting sky
with baptisms of dark cowling the woods
hidden minsters of peace

Winter Music

The windy winter trees
Fling their ghastly branches
To the night's roaring mystery,
To the day's dreary death;
Multi-coloured lights are prickling
On the black horizon, proudly staring
Into the moonless sky and the sound
Of the hungry wind is shrieking
In my ears as it gallops sea-crazy
Through the dusky darkness.

I sit enveloped in moody melancholy,
Mutely surrendering to the summer's decline,
For so the blackhearted night seems to sing;
Vagrant strands of sadness are webbing
Around the walls of my former happiness,
Threading the future with filaments
Of summer's shroud.

How can so much sadness spring from
A life of so much joy?
Life is not a simple thing –
It's an elaborate music played
On the nerves of experience,
Music of love and grief and joy ...
Inevitably the years bring notes of sadness
And the music keeps going out of key,
But there are always echoes
Of what used to be
And might be again.

Words of Love

You appeared in my life
As the realisation of a thousand dreams;
I was looking for you
And you found me;
Some element in the chemistry of our lives
Has drawn us fatefully, inevitably together;
The things that drew me to you are
The sound of your voice,
A note in your laugh,
The look of your face,
The shape of your body,
The way you walk;
But even more, an indefinable vibration
From inside you that touched
The innermost strings of my soul,
And made them respond with magic music,
Sounds too sweet and mysterious for words,
Sounds distilled by memories
And imaginings of you
Which when I am without you
Fill me also with such sadness
That my soul is split in two;
Love can be the only force
That in fusing me with you
Has divided me in two;
But if I were to lose you,
I would feel not divided but half-dead;
Love is the only name I can give
To the current that flows through me
When I think or dream of you;

Love is the only name I can give
To the desire your body fills me with,
The delight of touching you,
Ecstasy of being one with you;
I hope you can read between the lines,
For how can words describe
A sunrise or a rose?
I would prefer to write these words
With my lips and fingertips
On the lovely vellum of your skin –
Then I'm sure you would feel in your heart,
In each rhythm of your body's pleasure,
The full meaning and the melody,
The drumbeat and the rhapsody.

Zinjanthropus (Song of the Nutcracker Man)

I wonder if in some distant year
    I will soar above the now green and yellow land,
Will see the river-ribbons roving,
    The mountain tops,
The clouds and gilded sun giving birth
    To morning.

Or drift my days beneath the oceans,
    Ply there the colours of the rainbow quavering,
See the water-wonders weaving,
    Sailing fish,
The edges of my now world turned
    To trembling.

Maybe I will dwell among the trees,
    Know the forest haunts light and leafy darkening,
Watch the autumn-auburn awning,
    Fleeting deer,
The chants and hush folding of the green
    To evening.

I wonder if in that virgin year
    I will voyage the now pale and misty stars,
Know the forest and bright blood spill there,
    Unspill the ocean's spectral mysteries,
Unleash in the eye of the unsuspecting gull
    His surefire death;
Will I prise from its bed the cowering sea
    And stride leaden-hearted across the other worlds,
Trample on all dreaming, see my soul shorn
    To her last vibrancy?

And when no stone is left upon stone,
    Will I gaze at the rubble of my words,
Behold the gull plunging through ash-filled skies
    And my own uncomprehending eyes dimmed
To mourning? Ecce homo!

Have you read Eugene's novel **GHOSTERS**? It's about Frank Walsh, who is twelve years old when he enters a Roman Catholic seminary to fulfil his dream of becoming a priest. At twenty-one, having lost his faith, he makes an unsuccessful attempt to commit suicide, leaves the seminary and returns home. With the help of Sally, the girl next door, he slowly manages to recover from depression and starts to feel 'normal' again, especially sexually. After finishing university, he leaves home yet again – and Sally – to go and live in London. There he tries to escape the ghosts of his past and fulfil his dream of being a writer. He meets Marina, a vibrant Yugoslav girl, with whom he has a passionate love affair. They plan to marry, but a chance meeting with a ghost from the past threatens to destroy this dream too. Yet Frank refuses to be beaten, because he still has one dream left …

This is what Kate Cruise O'Brien, an editor at Poolbeg Press Ltd, wrote about Ghosters:

'I like it…imaginatively strong…I was riveted…sensitively worked out…intelligently written…powerfully presented…this heart-felt painful re-creation of a central hidden part of our culture.'

Ghosters is available from amazon.co.uk

OPPOSITE WORLDS is the sequel to Ghosters. It finds Frank alone and lonely in London, having been jilted by his Yugoslav girlfriend on their wedding day. On the rebound from this, he has a passionate affair with Kalli, a gorgeous Greek singer and belly-dancer, who is a student in his class at the school in Soho where he teaches English to foreign students. When Kalli leaves him, however, Frank is once again left alone and lonely. Then one evening, in a folk club in an Irish pub, he hears a young, attractive girl singing an Irish folk song and falls instantly in love with her. Her name is Mary, he contrives to meet her and Mary falls madly in love with him. Love leads to marriage – reluctantly at first on Frank's part – but their marriage proves to be a collision of two very different worlds …

'I read it with great enjoyment. Couldn't put it down.' John Barber

Opposite Worlds is available from amazon.com

You can get in touch with Eugene at:
eugenevesey@ntlworld.com

Printed in Great Britain
by Amazon

12899863R00087